HANK AARON
BRAVE IN EVERY WAY

PETER GOLENBOCK

Illustrated by
PAUL LEE

Clarion Books
An Imprint of HarperCollins*Publishers*
Boston New York

Clarion Books
An Imprint of HarperCollins Publishers, registered in the United States of America
and/or other jurisdictions.

www.clarionbooks.com

The Library of Congress has cataloged the hardcover edition as follows:
Golenbock, Peter, 1946– .
Hank Aaron: brave in every way/by Peter Golenbock; illustrated by Paul Lee.
p. cm.
Summary: A biography of the Hall of Fame baseball player who broke Babe Ruth's
career home run record.
1. Aaron, Hank, 1934—Juvenile literature.   2. Baseball players—United States—
Biography—Juvenile literature.   [1. Aaron, Hank, 1934– .   2. Baseball players.
3. Afro-Americans—Biography.]   I. Lee, Paul, ill.   II. Title.
GV865.A25G64   2001
796.357'092—dc21   00-8855
ISBN 0-15-202093-4
ISBN 0-15-205250-X pb

LEO   20 19

The illustrations in this book were done in acrylics on Bristol board.
The display type was set in Champion.
The text type was set in Goudy.
Printed and bound by Leo, China
Production supervision by Sandra Grebenar and Pascha Gerlinger
Designed by Ivan Holmes

To my son, Charlie,
who is wonderful in every way
—P. G.

To my mother,
who was brave in her own way
—P. L.

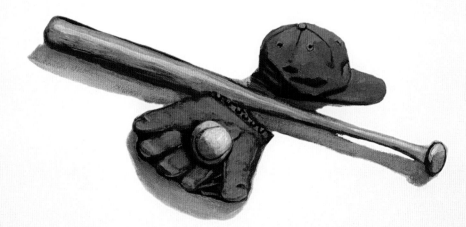

FROM THE MOMENT Hank Aaron was born, on February 5, 1934, his father, Herbert, wanted him to know the joy of playing baseball in open grassy fields, and his mother, Estella, dreamed that one day he would make a difference in the world.

It was the time of the Great Depression, and like millions of others, Herbert Aaron had great difficulty finding work. He had saved enough to buy some open country land just outside Mobile, Alabama, but he didn't have the money to buy a house, or even the wood to build one.

Hank was eight before his dad was finally able to build a small home for his family with the used boards from a torn-down house. The new house had no lights and no windowpanes. It had no bathroom. It had no refrigerator. But inside the Aaron house there was plenty of love. And nearby, in a pecan grove, was an open field for playing ball.

Hank loved living in the country, and he loved playing ball. There were days in school when Hank could think of nothing else. He would stare out the window, wishing he were on the ball field.

But his mama had her heart set on Hank going to college. "Hank, try to be the best," she would say. "Set goals for yourself and don't let anyone stop you from achieving them."

Hank's goal was to be a major-league ballplayer. Though his father didn't want to discourage Hank, he wanted him to be realistic. "There aren't any colored players in the major leagues," he reminded Hank.

It was true. Blacks were prohibited from playing in the major leagues. But that didn't stop Hank from dreaming. And America was beginning to change. The year Hank turned thirteen, Jackie Robinson joined the Brooklyn Dodgers. Major League Baseball had its first black player, and Robinson quickly became a star.

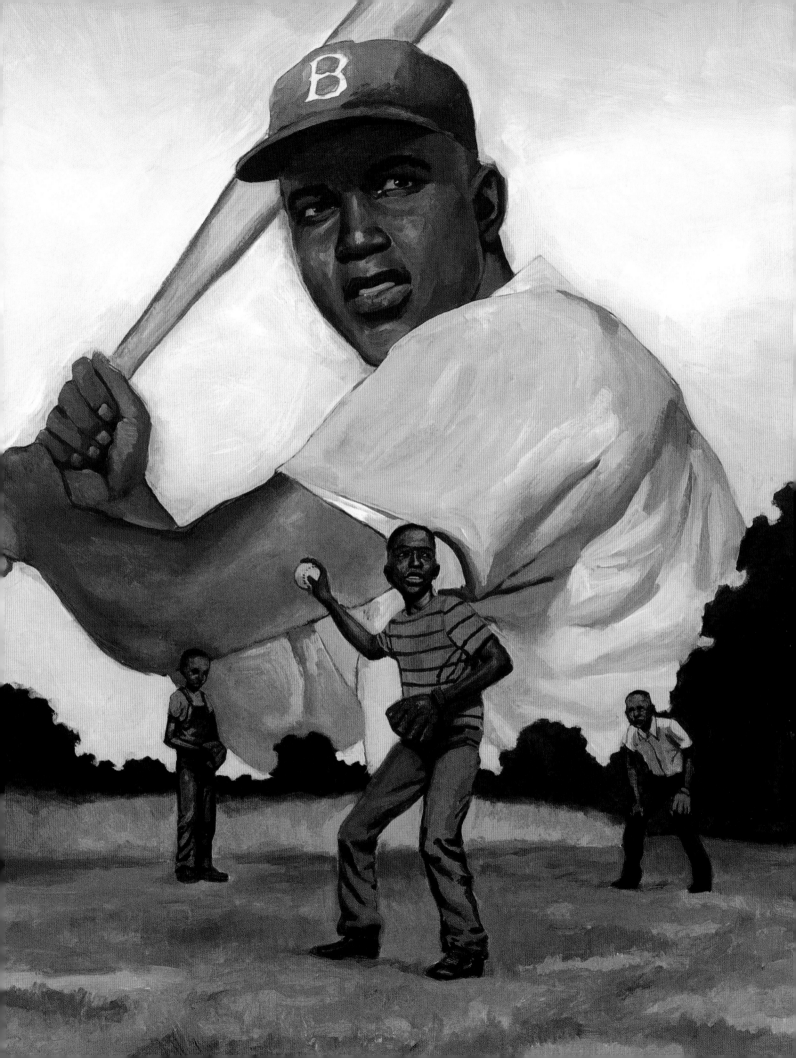

Hank studied. But he also played. And he was good. So good that when he had just turned sixteen, he was offered ten dollars a game to play shortstop for a local team called the Black Bears. Hank was afraid his mama wouldn't let him play. The Black Bear players were grown men. And worse still, the team played on Sundays, the holy day of rest. He was sure his mama would object.

But Hank wanted to play with the Black Bears more than anything. So he put his fears away and asked permission.

To his surprise, his mama came up with a compromise. He had to stay in school during the week and get his diploma. And she wouldn't let him travel with the team or be paid on Sunday, but he could play in every home game.

During his first year with the Black Bears, Hank displayed his extraordinary talents. He hit for a high average, was fleet on the bases, fielded well, and showed a strong throwing arm. He even hit some home runs. After a second season with the Black Bears, Hank was offered a job playing far from home for a professional team called the Indianapolis Clowns.

Hank's mama didn't understand how becoming a baseball player could help her son make a difference in the world. But she had faith in Hank and she saw that he loved the game.

So Estella made Hank a couple of sandwiches and stuffed two dollars into his pocket. Too upset to go to the train station to see him off, she stood in the yard crying as Hank left. "Your dad and I will be thinking of you always," she told him. "Be strong, son."

Hank Aaron *was* strong, and he soon impressed everyone with his talent. Wherever he played, Hank became a star.

Then, in 1954, Hank joined the Milwaukee Braves. He had done what he had dreamed of. He had made the major leagues.

Hank soon established himself as one of the leading home run hitters in the game. In 1956 he became the second youngest player ever to win a National League batting title. In 1957 and 1958 his powerful hitting led the Braves to league championships.

Hank remembered his father's determination and his mama's advice: Be the best you can be and keep your eyes on the goal. He became hungrier to excel. He decided to try to break the career home run record of Babe Ruth, baseball's most beloved hero.

When the Braves moved from Milwaukee to Atlanta, Georgia, in 1966, it helped Hank. He found it easy to hit home runs in the cozy Atlanta Stadium. And he was happy to be close to home.

But some people resented Hank's success because of the color of his skin. He began to get one or two unsigned letters each week filled with insults and nasty names.

your assault,
it's too late!
do not retire
baseball seen
family wi
great bit
Hate You!
You!
Quit or
Your Dea
P.S
Aaron:
Yankee fans. Which
we like Babe Ruth. Which
we do
You!
Hate
HANK AARON,
RETIRE OR DIE!
BE MOVING AROUN
Aaron Stinking Bla
read an article fr
ing kind of tough
better watch it, or
to retire NOW.
Brave
to
yours
late!
ll seen
of trouble

By the end of 1972, Hank was only forty-one home runs shy of the mighty Babe's 714, the most revered record in all of American sports. Hank was excited, but he was getting more and more angry letters claiming that a black man should not be challenging the record of a white man.

Hank decided to fight the best way he could. He swore that each angry letter would add a home run to his record.

When the new season started in 1973, Babe Ruth's sacred record lay ahead. The hate mail now arrived in torrents. Hank even got death threats. But Hank Aaron refused to allow anyone or anything to stop him.

And something remarkable happened that spring. The nation's newspapers began running stories telling about the hate mail. A chorus of well-wishers wrote Hank almost a million letters to offer him support. Throughout his life, Hank had had the support of his mother and father. But now a whole country of fans cheered for him.

Hank finished the '73 season with 713 home runs, just one behind Babe Ruth. In Atlanta, on the final day of the season, the appreciative fans rose and gave him a five-minute standing ovation.

Hank's next season began on the road, in Cincinnati. The entire nation was watching. In the very first game, Hank hit home run number 714 off pitcher Jack Billingham. He was tied with the Babe. From now on, every home run would set a new record.

When the Braves returned to Atlanta, the governor of the state of Georgia and the mayor of Atlanta were in the stands to watch Hank. So were Hank's mother and father. They had been his inspiration. They had taught him well. Hank was happy to know they were there.

In the fourth inning, two were out, a runner was on first. Hank watched as Dodger pitcher Al Downing threw a pitch low and down the middle. Hank swung.

The ball rocketed just over the head of the shortstop. It kept rising and rising until it sailed over the top of the high wall in left field and landed in the Braves' bull pen for home run number 715.

Lights flashed and fans cheered. Estella Aaron felt fear as well as joy. She remembered the hate mail and the death threats. What if someone tried to stop Hank from reaching home plate? As Hank passed second base, a couple of fans raced out of the stands to congratulate him. As he rounded third and headed for home, the entire Braves team rushed out to home plate to greet him. As he trotted toward home, his teammates parted for a waiting Estella Aaron.

When Hank touched the plate, his mama threw her arms around her boy. Hank was surprised his mama was hugging him so hard. When she was sure he was safe, she finally let go.

On this glorious day, before an entire nation, her son Hank had fulfilled his dreams.

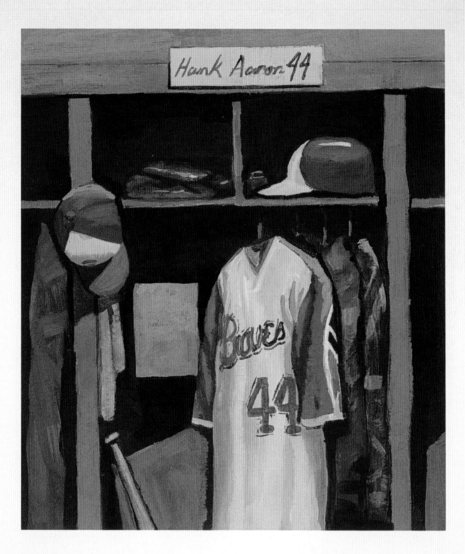

That night, when he was alone at last, Hank got down on his knees, closed his eyes, and thanked God for pulling him through.